THE
HUMAN BODY
IN 30 SECONDS

D1628412

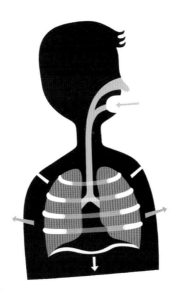

0 028 755 67X

First published in the UK in 2014 by

Ivy Press

210 High Street

Lewes

East Sussex BN7 2NS

United Kingdom

www.ivypress.co.uk

Copyright © 2014 Ivy Press Limited

All rights reserved. No part of this book may
be reproduced or transmitted in any form or by
any means, electronic or mechanical, including
photocopying, recording, or by any information
storage-and-retrieval system, without written
permission from the copyright holder.

978-1-78240-147-6

This book was conceived, designed and produced by

Ivy Press

CREATIVE DIRECTOR	Peter Bridgewater
PUBLISHER	Susan Kelly
COMMISSIONING EDITOR	Hazel Songhurst
MANAGING EDITOR	Hazel Songhurst
PROJECT EDITOR	Judith Chamberlain-Webber
ART DIRECTOR	Kim Hankinson
DESIGNER	Hanri Shaw
ILLUSTRATOR	Wesley Robins

Printed in China

Colour origination by Ivy Press Reprographics

10 9 8 7 6 5 4 3 2 1

THE
HUMAN BODY

IN 30 SECONDS

SEFTON LIBRARY SERVICES	
002875567	
1442468/00	25/11/2014
J612	CLA
CROS	£9.99

ANNA CLAYBOURNE

Ivy Kids

Contents

About this book
... in 60 seconds

The human body is an amazing, living, breathing, incredibly complex machine – and we all have one of our very own!

Wherever you are, and whatever you're doing, your body is where you live – 24 hours a day, every day of your life. It has senses to tell you what's going on around you, a brain for thinking and making decisions, and muscles so that you can move. It takes in food and oxygen, and turns them into the energy you need to keep going.

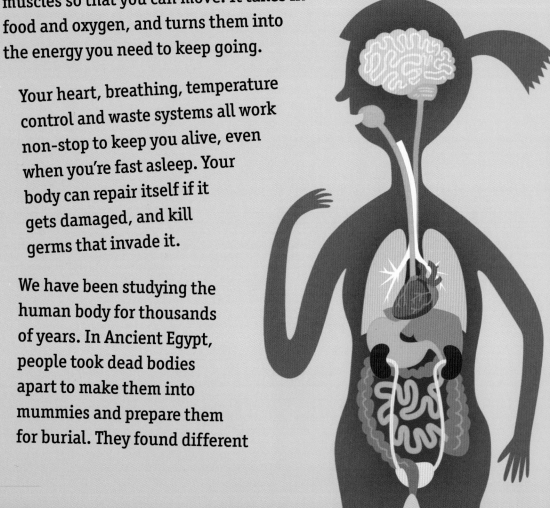

Your heart, breathing, temperature control and waste systems all work non-stop to keep you alive, even when you're fast asleep. Your body can repair itself if it gets damaged, and kill germs that invade it.

We have been studying the human body for thousands of years. In Ancient Egypt, people took dead bodies apart to make them into mummies and prepare them for burial. They found different organs and body bits, such as the lungs, brain and appendix. Since then, we've learnt about what most of our body parts do.

However, we are still finding out new things. Less than 100 years ago, scientists discovered how DNA, a chemical found inside our cells, controls how our bodies work and grow. Less than ten years ago, we finally worked out that toes and fingertips wrinkle in the bath to give us a better grip on wet surfaces! Some things, such as how the brain allows us to think, are still a mystery.

The chapters in this book explore all the body's building blocks, organs and amazing abilities. Each of the 30 topics has a speedy explanation to read, along with a super-snappy 3-second sum-up. The 3-minute missions have experiments you can try to test your own body, so you can see for yourself how your amazing body works!

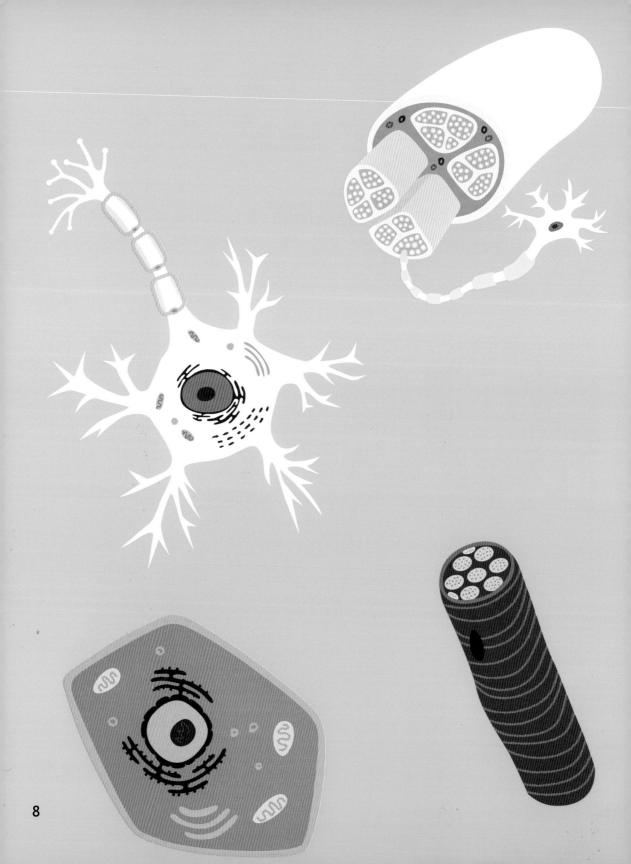

8

Body bits

Compared to a mountain, a tower block or even an elephant, you might feel quite small. But you are actually a very large, complicated living thing, made up of millions of different working parts. Like other living things, the human body is made of tiny cells. They link together to form body tissues such as skin and muscle, organs such as your stomach and brain, and body systems, such as the digestive system.

Body bits
Glossary

amoeba A type of organism with one **cell**. Most have no hard parts and look like blobs of jelly.

axon The long thread part of a nerve cell along which messages are passed.

bacterium (plural: bacteria) A type of tiny living thing that has just one cell. Some bacteria cause disease, such as food poisoning.

body tissue Part of the body of a living thing that is made of similar **cells**, such as the cardiac tissue of your heart.

cell One of the tiny units that living things are made of. Some organisms, such as **bacteria**, are made up of a single cell, while others are made up of trillions of cells.

cortex The outer layer of the brain, which plays an important role in thinking.

cytoplasm The fluid that fills a **cell**.

digest To break food down so your body can use it.

gene A section of a DNA strand inside a cell **nucleus**, which contains instructions for cells to follow.

membrane A thin layer of skin-like tissue found in various parts of the body.

nerve Enclosed bundles of long fibres, made up of nerve cells. They carry communication signals around the body.

neuron One of the billions of nerve cells that make up the nervous system and carry electrical signals at high speed.

nucleus The core at the centre of a **cell**. It acts like the brain of the cell and controls the way the cell works.

organ A body part, such as the heart, that is made of two or more tissues and has one or more specific roles.

organelle One of several 'little organs' inside a **cell** that has a specific job, e.g. the **nucleus**.

vitamin A natural substance found in food that you need to help you grow and stay healthy.

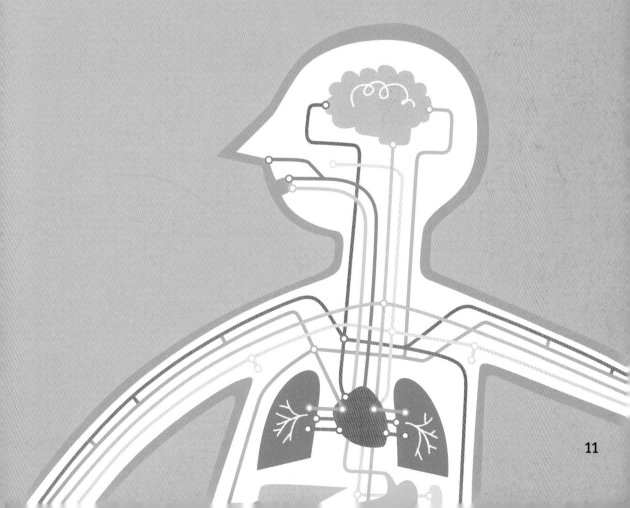

Cells

... in 30 seconds

Cells are very small – so tiny that most of them can only be seen under a microscope. Each cell has its own protective skin, or cell membrane, filled with watery, jelly-like cytoplasm. Floating in the cytoplasm are the cell's own mini-organs, called organelles.

Most cells have a headquarters, called the nucleus. In here are the genes that control what the cell does and how it works. A few types of cells, though, such as red blood cells, don't have a nucleus, because they don't need one.

The cells in the human body are not all the same. In fact, you have around 200 different types of cells, all adapted for doing different jobs. For example, red blood cells carry oxygen, skin cells form layers of skin, and special brain and nerve cells, called neurons, carry signals around the body.

As well as doing their own jobs, cells can communicate, work together in groups, and stick together to form larger body parts.

3-second sum-up

The human body is made up of trillions of tiny cells.

How many cells?

How many cells do living things have? There are too many to count, so scientists calculate the numbers based on body weight and type.

• Many creatures, such as bacteria and amoebas, have one cell.

• A tiny fruit fly has around a million cells.

• Humans have around 50–100 trillion cells.

• A large elephant could have over a quadrillion cells (that's a thousand trillion, or 1,000,000,000,000,000).

Your cells look very different depending on what job they do.

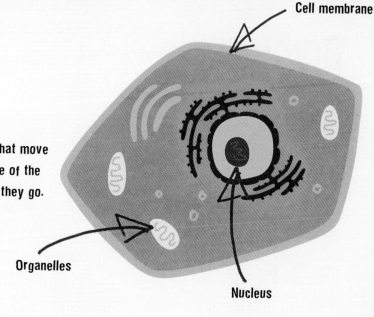

Cell membrane

Skin cells form layers that move up towards the surface of the skin, getting flatter as they go.

Organelles

Nucleus

Dendrites (branches)

Nucleus

Cell body

Muscle cells are long rod-like shapes that contract (get shorter) to make the whole muscle contract.

Muscle fibre

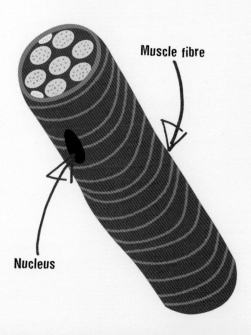

Axon

Nerve cells carry information around the brain and body through their tree-like branches.

Nucleus

Body tissues

... in 30 seconds

When you look at part of your body, such as your hand, hair or tongue, you're looking at millions and millions of cells, all stuck together to make body tissues.

If cells didn't stick together like this, you wouldn't have a body! You'd just be a pile of cells on the floor, and would look pretty much like soup.

Cells form several different types of tissues:

• **Skin** Cells form skin to cover your body and your organs, such as your heart and stomach. Skin-like tissues line the insides of organs too, such as the intestines. Skin cells also form hair and nail tissue.

• **Muscles** These are also a type of body tissue, made up of millions of muscle cells. There are muscles all over your skeleton, and more making up parts of organs, such as your stomach, eyes and heart.

• **Nerve tissue** This makes up the nerve pathways that reach all through your body and brain to carry signals between body parts.

• **Connective tissue** This is tough tissue that holds body bits together. For example, it holds your skin onto your body.

3-second sum-up

Cells stick together to form tissues that make body parts.

3-minute mission Take a closer look!

You need: • A hand-held microscope or magnifying glass

You can't see many of your body tissues because they are hidden inside you. Use the magnifying glass or microscope to get a good look at your skin, hair and fingernails. What do they look like close up? Take a picture!

The different types of tissues in your body are made from different kinds of cells.

Skin is made up of layer upon layer of skin cells. The cells forming the outer layer are dead.

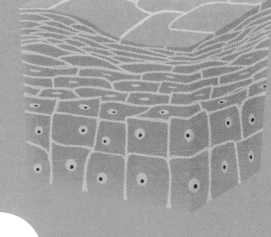

Nerves carrying signals around the body are made up of strands of tightly packed nerve cells.

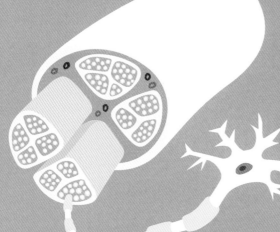

Skeletal muscles are made up of groups of muscle cells arranged in tube-like clusters.

Organs
... in 30 seconds

When you need to think, you use your brain. To breathe in, you use your lungs; and to see, you use your eyes.

These are all organs – body parts for doing particular jobs. Organs are usually made up of several different types of cells and tissues. Altogether, you have around 80 of them.

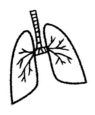

The most complicated organ is the brain. As well as the cortex, or thinking part, it has several other parts that deal with storing memories, helping you balance, and controlling your breathing and heartbeat. The brain has more than 100 billion cells!

Many other organs are simpler, and do just one task. The eyes collect light patterns from outside your body to send to the brain. The stomach dissolves and mushes up your food. The bladder is a stretchy bag for storing urine (wee) until you go to the toilet.

Some organs do lots of jobs. The liver, the biggest organ of all, has around 500 jobs! They include storing vitamins, making chemicals that digest food and storing energy for your cells to use.

3-minute mission Organ quiz

Match the organ to the job! Check on the Internet if you want.

Organ	Job
Kidney	Traps germs
Heart	Makes voice sounds
Oesophagus	Pumps blood
Lung	Filters waste out of blood
Lymph node	Extracts oxygen from air
Larynx	Carries food from throat to stomach

3-second sum-up

Organs are complex body parts that do particular jobs.

Answer on page 96

Organs are made from specific cells and tissues that help them do their jobs.

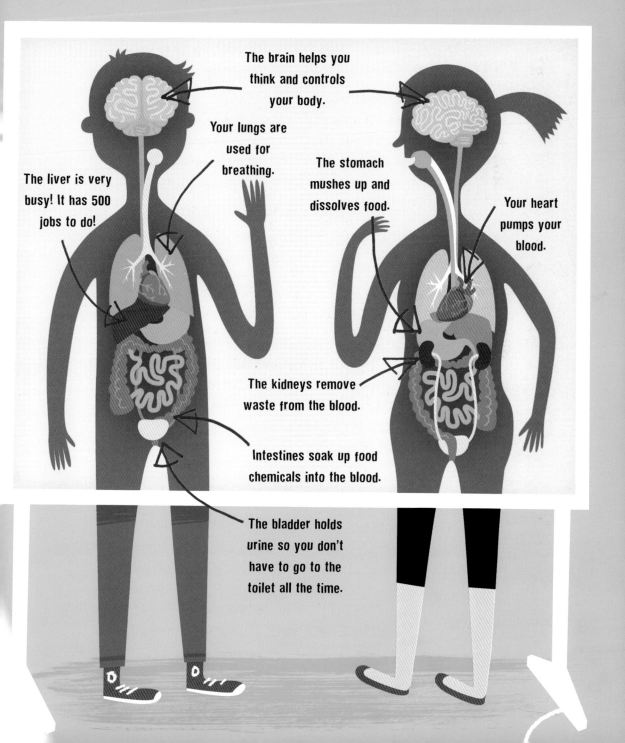

The brain helps you think and controls your body.

Your lungs are used for breathing.

The stomach mushes up and dissolves food.

Your heart pumps your blood.

The liver is very busy! It has 500 jobs to do!

The kidneys remove waste from the blood.

Intestines soak up food chemicals into the blood.

The bladder holds urine so you don't have to go to the toilet all the time.

Body systems
... in 30 seconds

Your body is a bit like a big, busy city, with lots of activities going on all at once. There are several separate systems to make everything run smoothly.

A city has a transport system, food and energy supply systems, and systems for waste disposal, carrying messages and dealing with danger. The body is the same. Groups of cells, tissues and organs work together to run your body.

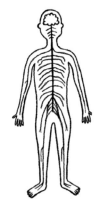

For example, the digestive system deals with food. The mouth takes in and chews food, the throat swallows it and the oesophagus carries it to the stomach. The stomach mushes the food, then the small intestine soaks up the useful chemicals, and the large intestine collects the leftovers.

The nervous system is the body's message system, carrying signals between the sense organs, the brain and the muscles. The circulatory system (heart, blood and blood vessels) is the transport network, carrying oxygen, food chemicals and medicines to wherever they are needed. The immune system is like a police force, guarding against germs.

3-second sum-up

Body tissues and organs work in groups to form body systems.

Connected systems

If you could look inside your body, you wouldn't see lots of neat, separate body systems – you'd see a tangled jumble of tubes, organs and tissues. The body systems are all connected and entangled with each other, and some body parts belong to more than one system. For example, your nose is used for both breathing (respiratory system) and smelling (nervous system).

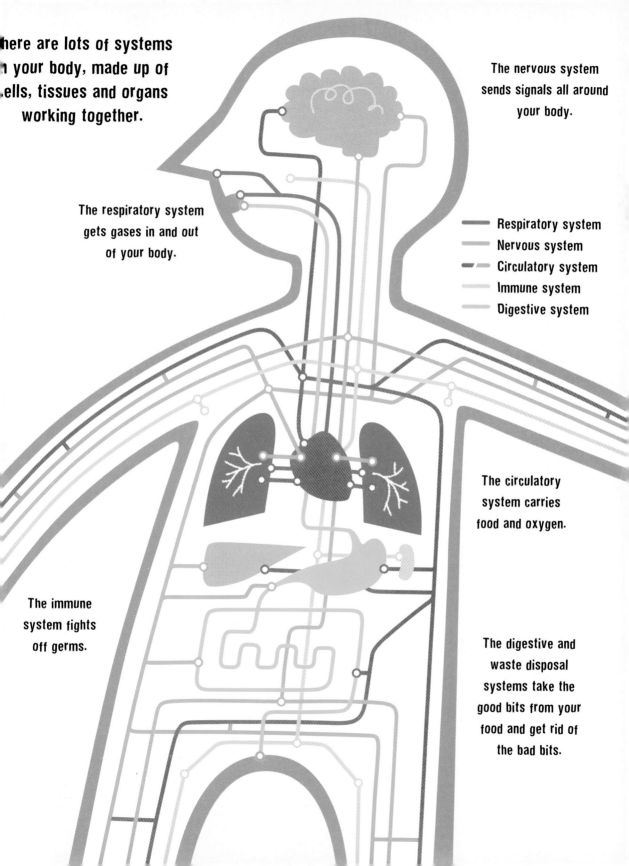

There are lots of systems in your body, made up of cells, tissues and organs working together.

The nervous system sends signals all around your body.

The respiratory system gets gases in and out of your body.

Respiratory system
Nervous system
Circulatory system
Immune system
Digestive system

The circulatory system carries food and oxygen.

The immune system fights off germs.

The digestive and waste disposal systems take the good bits from your food and get rid of the bad bits.

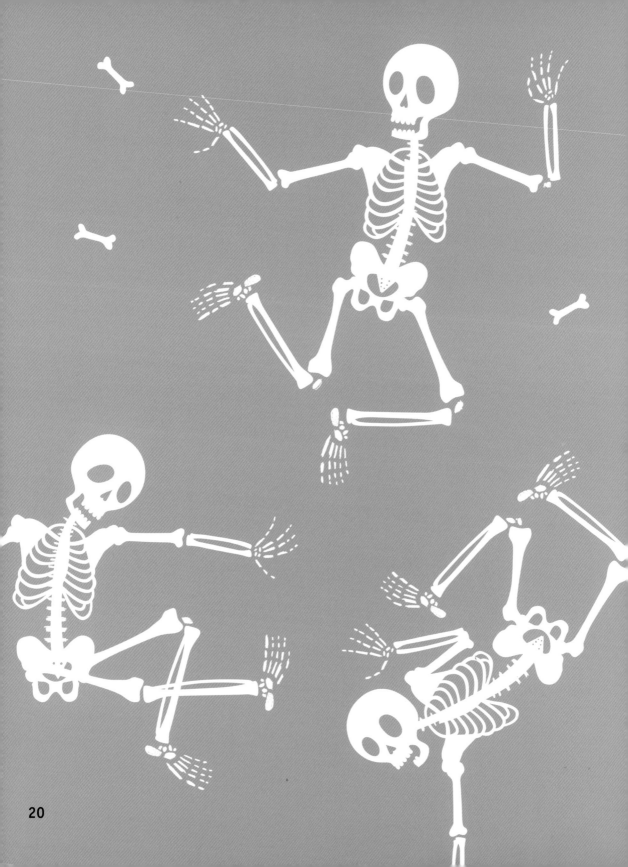

Body structure

Ask a friend to draw a person in three seconds flat, and they'll probably draw a simple stick figure with two arms, two legs, a body and a head. This basic shape, which we share with many other animals, is thanks to our skeleton. It forms a basic, jointed framework. Muscles attached all over it help us to make movements, while skin, hair and nails provide a protective covering.

Glossary

bacterium (plural: bacteria) A type of tiny living thing that has just one cell. Some bacteria cause illness, such as food poisoning.

biceps The large **muscle** at the front of your upper arm, which bends your forearm.

calcium A chemical element that is very important for the human body. It is used to build strong bones and teeth.

filament A tiny, thin, thread-like part found in **muscle** cells.

involuntary muscle A muscle that is controlled directly by the brain stem without you thinking about it, e.g. heart muscle.

keratin A fibre-like **protein** found in the outer layer of the skin and in hair and nails.

ligament A band of tough tissue that joins bones together between a joint.

marrow The innermost part of a bone. It looks like a thick jelly and its job is to make blood cells.

mineral A naturally occurring substance or element, such as **calcium**, that you need for your body to work properly. You get minerals from your food.

muscle A body part that contracts (gets shorter) to produce movement.

nerve Enclosed bundles of long fibres, made up of nerve cells. They carry communication signals around the body.

protein A substance made from tiny building blocks called amino acids. Proteins are a vital part of all living things.

reflex An involuntary, or automatic, action that your body does in response to something – without having to send a signal to the brain.

triceps The muscle on the back of your arm, which straightens your elbow.

Bones

... in 30 seconds

What would you be without your skeleton? You'd be a soft, shapeless, blobby bag of organs, in a heap on the floor, that's what!

Your skeleton is your body's framework. Because bones are hard and strong, they can hold you up and give you your shape and structure. Some bones, such as the skull and ribs, have another job too – they protect soft organs such as the brain, heart and lungs. Bones also store important minerals.

The skeleton is made up of over 200 bones, linked together by moving joints. This means it can move into thousands of different positions, so you can walk and run, talk and chew, pick up a pen, do a handstand or scratch your nose.

When you think of a skeleton, you probably think of old, dried-out bones. But, when you are alive, your bones are alive too. They are complex body parts with their own nerves and blood vessels running through them, connecting them to the rest of the body. Large bones also have a soft substance called bone marrow inside them. Bone marrow does the vital job of making new blood cells for the body.

3-second sum-up

The skeleton holds the body up, protects organs and helps you move.

3-minute mission Rubber bone

You need: • Cooked and cooled, clean, dry chicken bone • Jar • White vinegar

Bones are hard because they contain a lot of the mineral calcium. To see what would happen without it, put the bone in the vinegar and leave it to soak for a few days. The vinegar removes the calcium, making the bone soft and rubbery.

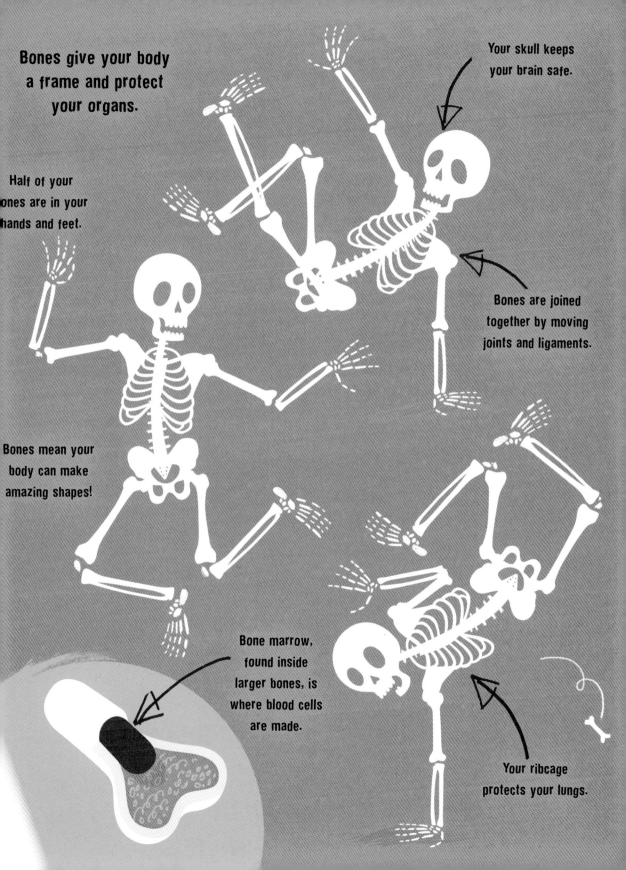

Bones give your body
a frame and protect
your organs.

Your skull keeps
your brain safe.

Half of your
bones are in your
hands and feet.

Bones are joined
together by moving
joints and ligaments.

Bones mean your
body can make
amazing shapes!

Bone marrow,
found inside
larger bones, is
where blood cells
are made.

Your ribcage
protects your lungs.

Muscles

... in 30 seconds

To stay alive, your body has to move. Walking, eating, speaking – even breathing – can only happen because of the muscles that move body parts around.

If you squeeze your upper arm or your calf, you'll feel muscles under your skin. These are the skeletal muscles – muscles that are attached to your bones. There are about 640 of them, all over your skeleton. They link bones together to pull them into different positions.

Many organs, such as the stomach and intestines, have to move to work. They use a type of muscle called smooth muscle, which forms stretchy loops or bands inside or around body parts. There are millions of these muscles, including one attached to each of your 5 million body hairs! The heart has a special type of muscle, called cardiac muscle.

Muscles work by pulling. A muscle can contract, or get shorter, which makes it pull on whatever it's attached to, or squeeze whatever it's wrapped around. When the muscle relaxes, it gets longer again.

3-second sum-up

Muscles pull on body parts to make them move.

Goosebumps!

Being cold or scared can cause goosebumps. This makes animals look bigger and scarier, or keep warm, by making their hair stand on end. Humans no longer have such long body hair, but we still get goosebumps! Next time you get them, look closely. You'll see each body hair standing up, pulling the skin into a bump. Each hair has a tiny bundle of smooth muscle that can pull it upright.

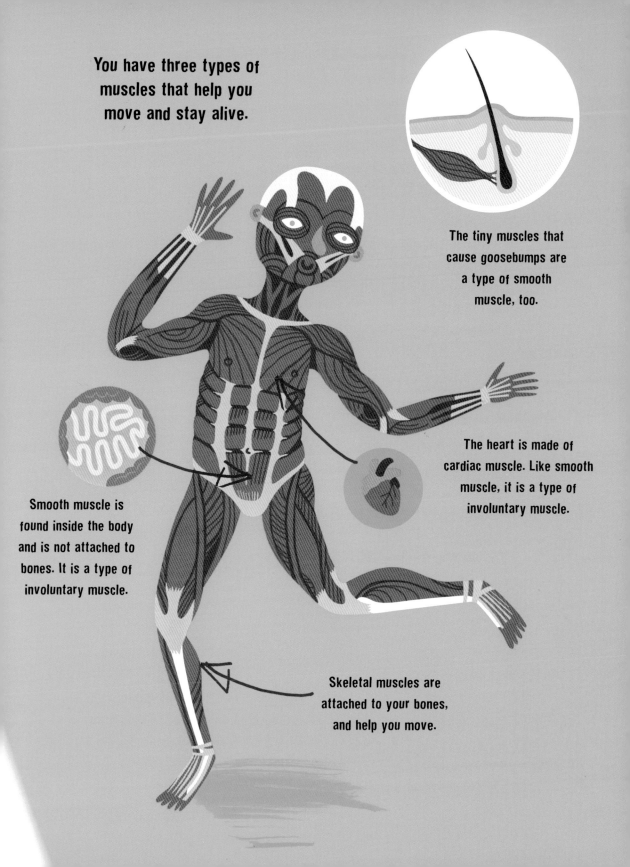

You have three types of
muscles that help you
move and stay alive.

The tiny muscles that
cause goosebumps are
a type of smooth
muscle, too.

The heart is made of
cardiac muscle. Like smooth
muscle, it is a type of
involuntary muscle.

Smooth muscle is
found inside the body
and is not attached to
bones. It is a type of
involuntary muscle.

Skeletal muscles are
attached to your bones,
and help you move.

Movement

... in 30 seconds

Someone offers you an ice cream, so you reach out your arm to take one. What is actually happening to make you move?

Muscle cells contain two types of stringy muscle filaments, called actin and myosin, that overlap each other. To make the muscle contract, the brain sends it a signal. This makes the actin and myosin filaments overlap more tightly and pull together. The muscle gets shorter and thicker, making it bulge as it pulls two body parts towards each other.

To stretch out your arm, your brain sends a signal to the triceps muscle. This muscle links the shoulder blade and the back of the upper arm bone to the back of the elbow. As the triceps shortens, it pulls the elbow up, making your arm straighten.

But what next? You now need to get the ice cream to your mouth, and muscles can only pull. To bend your arm back again, the triceps relaxes, and another muscle, the biceps, takes over. The biceps links the shoulder blade and the front of the upper arm bone to both the bones of the forearm. When it contracts, it pulls the forearm up, and your arm bends.

3-second sum-up

Muscles work in pairs to make body parts move to and fro.

3-minute mission Test your reflexes

Reflexes are movements that you make automatically. The kneejerk reflex is the best-known – try yours! Sit with your legs crossed and ask a friend to tap you just below the knee with a ruler or the edge of a book. What happens to your leg? It should swing up. The signal doesn't come from your brain, but from your spinal cord, in response to something happening to your body.

Your nervous system and muscles work together to make you move.

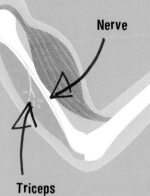

Nerve

Triceps

Your brain sends a signal along your nerves to your triceps muscle.

The muscle filaments tighten, the triceps shortens and your arm straightens.

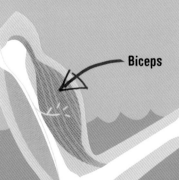

Signals to finger muscles make them curl around your target. Got it!

Biceps

Now the brain sends signals to your biceps muscle.

The filaments tighten, the biceps shortens and your arm bends.

Now you can eat your ice cream!

Teeth
... in 30 seconds

You can't see most of your skeleton. But look in the mirror, smile, and there's one bit you can see – your teeth!

Teeth aren't bones, but they are similar. Each tooth has an outer covering of tough, shiny enamel – the hardest substance in the human body. Under that is the bone-like dentine, which contains a lot of calcium and other minerals. In the middle is the soft pulp, containing the blood vessels and nerves linking the tooth to the rest of the body. The tooth's long roots hold it in place in the jawbone.

Teeth are pretty important. As well as chewing food, they play a big part in speaking, and we also use them as tools for tearing or cutting things. Unlike bones, teeth can't repair themselves if they get damaged. The enamel is very strong, but it can be eaten away by acidic foods, and by bacteria that feed on old food. Brushing your teeth gets rid of these and keeps the enamel safe.

Bones grow, but teeth don't – they just push up through your gums. Babies have a set of 20 small 'milk teeth', which fall out to be replaced by 32 adult teeth as your mouth gets bigger.

3-second sum-up

Humans have 32 teeth for chewing food and making speech sounds.

3-minute mission Egg-speriment

Here's what fizzy drinks do to teeth:

1 Get two pale-coloured, hard-boiled eggs (ask an adult to boil and cool them). Put each egg in a cup of cola.

2 After a few minutes, take one out and brush it clean with a toothbrush and toothpaste.

3 Leave the other overnight. What do you see?

You have three types of teeth, which are set into your jawbone.

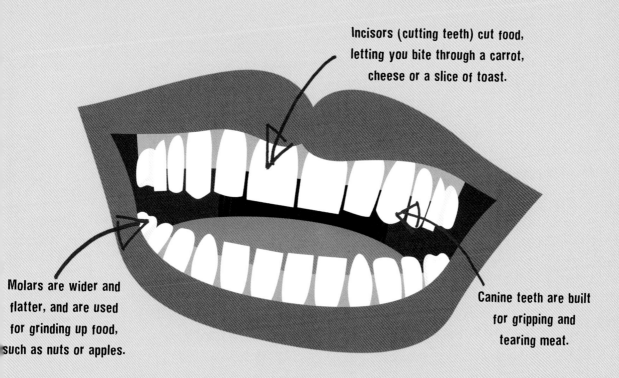

Incisors (cutting teeth) cut food, letting you bite through a carrot, cheese or a slice of toast.

Molars are wider and flatter, and are used for grinding up food, such as nuts or apples.

Canine teeth are built for gripping and tearing meat.

Inside a tooth

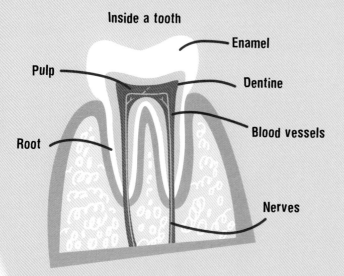

Pulp

Root

Enamel

Dentine

Blood vessels

Nerves

X-rays show how adult teeth queue up behind the milk teeth in a toddler, ready to take over.

Skin, hair and nails

... in 30 seconds

Skin is one of the biggest body parts of all. If you could take off an adult's skin and spread it out, it would take up about as much space as a single bed, and would weigh as much as three winter coats!

Skin does a lot of essential jobs for your body. These include:

Holding all your organs and body bits together

Keeping water in – skin is waterproof and stops your body drying out

Keeping water out! – skin stops you soaking up water like a sponge when you're in the bath or swimming

Keeping you warm – a layer of fat just under your skin keeps heat in

Keeping you cool — if you're too hot, your skin sweats to cool you down

Forming a barrier to keep dirt and germs out

Cushioning your bones and joints

Feeling pressure, heat, cold and pain, with touch-sensitive nerves.

Hair, fingernails and toenails grow out of the skin, and are all made of a protein called keratin. They are formed from skin-like cells and grow longer as the skin pushes them outwards.

3-second sum-up

Skin, hair and nails form the outer covering of the body.

3-minute mission How strong is your hair?

1 Gently pull out one hair, and tape it to the end of a pencil.

2 Use a pile of books to sandwich the other end of the pencil so that it sticks out with the hair dangling down.

3 Tape a penny onto the other end of the hair. Keep adding more pennies. How many can it hold before it snaps?

Skin, hair and nails protect your body from the outside world.

Skin, hair and nails are also the body bits that are on show all the time. So people decorate and jazz them up!

Eyebrows and eyelashes protect eyes from sweat, rain and dust.

Hair keeps your head warm.

When you dive into a swimming pool, your skin does almost all of its jobs.

Nails protect your sensitive fingertips.

Survival systems

You need a sandwich, and you need it now! Your body is brilliant at keeping itself going – you take in food and air to keep all your cells working and your energy levels up. All the time, your heart beats and pumps your blood, which flows all around your body to supply the cells with everything they need. Meanwhile, the immune system guards against germs and diseases.

Survival systems
Glossary

acid A type of strong chemical. Acid in the stomach helps to kill germs that may be in your food and dissolve food into a mush to be digested.

alveolus (plural: alveoli) A tiny air sac inside your lungs with a very thin wall that allows **oxygen** to be passed to red blood **cells**.

antibody A protein made by white blood **cells** that helps to fight off germs.

artery A blood vessel that carries blood from the heart to the rest of the body.

capillary A tiny blood vessel, with a wall one **cell** thick, which links **arteries** to **veins**.

carbon dioxide Waste gas made by body **cells** and carried to the lungs in the blood to be breathed out.

cell One of the tiny units that living things are made of. Some organisms, such as bacteria, are made up of a single cell, while others are made up of trillions of cells.

diaphragm A dome-shaped **muscle** that is just below the lungs. It goes down when you breathe in and up when you breathe out.

diarrhoea Watery poo that is more frequent or urgent than usual.

digest To break food down so your body can use it.

enzyme A special type of protein that helps produce and speed up chemical reactions.

gland An organ that produces a substance for the body to use.

intestine One of the long tubes in the digestive system that absorb the useful parts from food and collect waste.

lymph A colourless fluid that contains white blood **cells** and is found in your lymphatic system and lymph nodes.

muscle A body part that contracts (i.e. gets shorter) to produce movement.

nutrient A substance in food that the body can use to survive and grow.

oxygen A gas in the air that humans and other animals need to breathe.

saliva A liquid that is released from glands in the mouth to help you taste and dissolve food.

spleen A small organ between your stomach and **diaphragm** on the left-hand side of your body that helps to filter the blood and make new red blood **cells**.

urine (wee) A liquid made up of water and waste products, filtered out of the blood by the kidneys. Urine is stored in the bladder.

valve A structure that can open and close to make sure blood doesn't flow backwards.

vein A blood vessel that carries blood back to the heart.

villus (plural: villi) One of the tiny, finger-shaped parts of the small **intestine** through which digested food is absorbed.

vomiting Throwing up the contents of your stomach through your mouth.

Digestive system

... in 30 seconds

When you eat food, it goes through your digestive system. This is a passage leading right through your body, made up of several organs linked together. The food goes through five main stages...

Chewing You grind food into bits using your teeth. Your mouth releases saliva (spit) to make the food softer and help to dissolve it.

Swallowing Your tongue rolls the food to the back of your mouth. Strong muscles squeeze it down your throat into the oesophagus, a tube leading to your stomach.

Dissolving Your stomach squeezes and squishes the food, mixing it with strong stomach acid. This dissolves the food into a kind of runny soup.

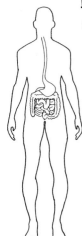

Absorbing The food soup is squirted into a long, coiled-up tube – the small intestine. It's lined with millions of tiny finger-shaped body parts called villi. They soak up useful chemicals and pass them into your blood.

Waste collection The leftover bits such as tomato seeds and tough sweetcorn skin pass into the large intestine and collect into lumps of poo, which finally leave your body when you go to the toilet.

3-second sum-up

The digestive system dissolves food, soaks up the good bits, then gets rid of the waste.

3-minute mission How long?

The digestive system isn't a straight line – it has lots of coils and loops, especially in the small intestine. In fact, your digestive system is about 4.5 times longer than you!

To see how long yours is, measure your height and multiply it by 4.5. Write down the answer and measure out a piece of string that long. Stretch it out on the floor, and you'll see how far your food travels!

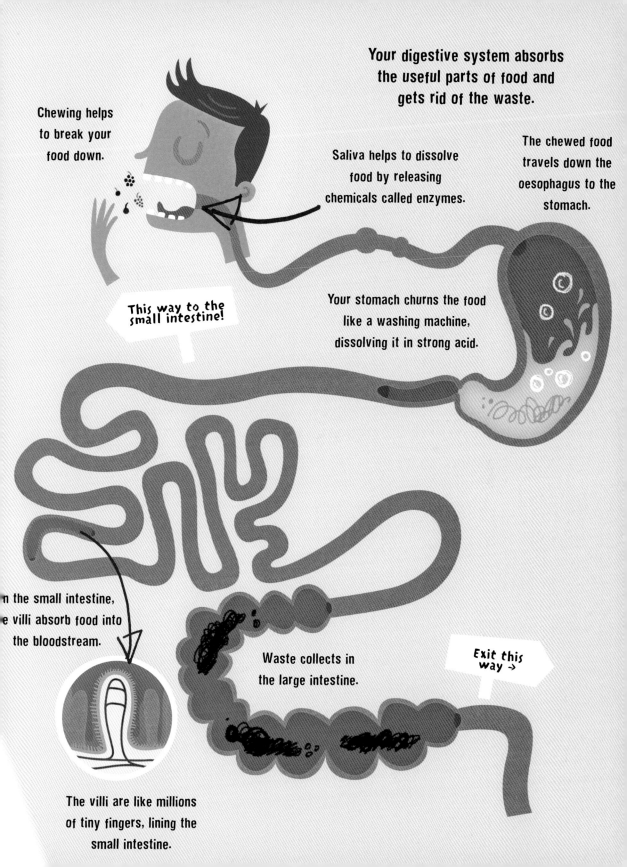

Waste

... in 30 seconds

Just like a big city, your body makes lots of waste. It has to be removed, or it would collect inside you and make you ill. Some waste comes out when you go to the toilet – but that's not the only kind. In fact, you leave waste everywhere you go!

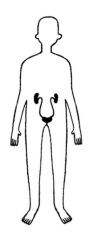

Poo is made of all the bits of food you can't digest. Each poo also contains some of the bacteria that live in your intestines.

Urine, or wee, is liquid waste. All the blood in your body passes through the two kidneys, which collect spare water and waste chemicals from it. They send the urine to your bladder to be stored, then let it out of your body several times a day.

Carbon dioxide is a waste gas that's made when cells turn food into energy. Your blood carries it to your lungs, and you breathe it out.

Cells in your body constantly die, and new ones are made to replace them. Some dead cells get taken to the spleen, where they are recycled. Some get eaten up by special blood cells. And dead skin cells simply flake off – up to 500 million of them a day!

3-second sum-up

Your body constantly makes and releases various different types of waste.

3-minute mission Weigh your skin dust!

Shedding a whopping 500 million skin cells a day adds up to about 200 billion a year! Those cells weigh an impressive 700 g (1½ lb) and make up a large part of the dust we find in the air and all around our homes. Yuck!

To find out how much skin dust you've made so far, multiply your age by 700 g (1½ lb). How much dust would you make in an average lifetime of 80 years?

The body systems collect, store and expel waste to keep your body clean and safe.

When you eat and drink, your body takes what it needs to make cells, muscles and other body parts work.

The bits that your body doesn't need have to be removed.

In one day, your body will get rid of...

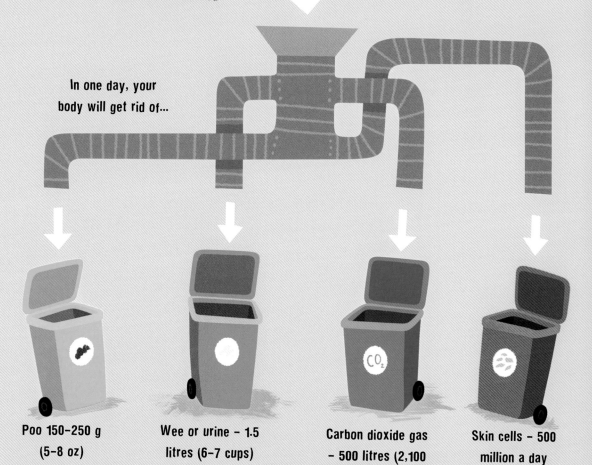

Poo 150–250 g (5–8 oz)

Wee or urine – 1.5 litres (6–7 cups)

Carbon dioxide gas – 500 litres (2,100 cups) – enough to fill 200 balloons

Skin cells – 500 million a day

Breathing

... in 30 seconds

All day and all night, whether you are thinking about it or not, you keep breathing.

Breathing is involuntary – you can do it without trying. However, you can also control it when you want to; for example, when you hold your breath, speak, sing or blow a musical instrument.

The body system that makes you breathe is called the respiratory system, and the main breathing organs are the two big, spongy, squishy lungs in your chest. When you breathe in, muscles in your chest make your lungs expand. They suck in air through your mouth and nose, and down your windpipe or trachea.

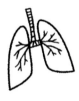

Inside each lung, the air flows down little tubes called bronchioles into about 300 million tiny bags – the alveoli. Oxygen from the air passes out through the alveoli walls and into the tiny blood vessels surrounding them. Then the blood carries the oxygen away to be used by all the body's cells.

At the same time, the blood drops off waste carbon dioxide gas collected from the cells back into the alveoli to be breathed out.

3-second sum-up

The lungs take in air to use the oxygen it contains.

Julius Caesar's breath

You may have heard that every time you breathe in, you take in some of the air molecules breathed out by the great Ancient Roman leader Julius Caesar. But it's not just Caesar – every time you breathe in, you take in air molecules breathed out by many people from the past! The countless gazillions of molecules floating around in the atmosphere are constantly being mixed up and breathed in and out by everyone.

You breathe using your lungs and chest muscles.

To breathe in, chest muscles pull your ribs up and out, and the diaphragm pulls down.

To breathe out, the chest muscles squeeze your lungs, and the diaphragm goes up.

Diaphragm muscle

Singing requires careful control of the breath. Your voice is your instrument!

An accordion sucks in air then blows it out, just like your lungs!

You have to take in extra deep breaths to blow a wind instrument.

Blood

... in 30 seconds

Blood is your body's delivery system. It flows all around your body, visiting every cell, tissue and organ. Blood carries oxygen, collected from your lungs, to all your cells. It also picks up food chemicals from your intestines, and carries them all over your body.

Blood delivers all kinds of other useful things, too. It collects waste products from cells and carries them away. Any medicines you take go into your blood, and are carried to where they are needed.

Blood also delivers hormones, chemicals that send messages from one body part to another. For example, when you feel in danger, glands near your kidneys release the hormone adrenaline into your blood. When the adrenaline reaches your heart, it makes it beat faster to give you extra energy and speed.

The heart pumps blood around the body through a huge network of tubes called blood vessels. As blood leaves the heart, it flows through big, wide blood vessels. They branch off into smaller and smaller tubes, and then into tiny capillaries that reach all your cells.

3-second sum-up

Blood flows all around your body, delivering oxygen, food and other useful substances.

Amazing blood facts

• One drop of blood contains over 300 million blood cells.

• An adult has about 5 litres (9 pints) of blood in total.

• Each person has about 100,000 km (60,000 miles) of blood vessels! The tiny capillaries make up most of the length.

• An individual blood cell takes about a minute to travel from the heart, around the body, and back to the heart again.

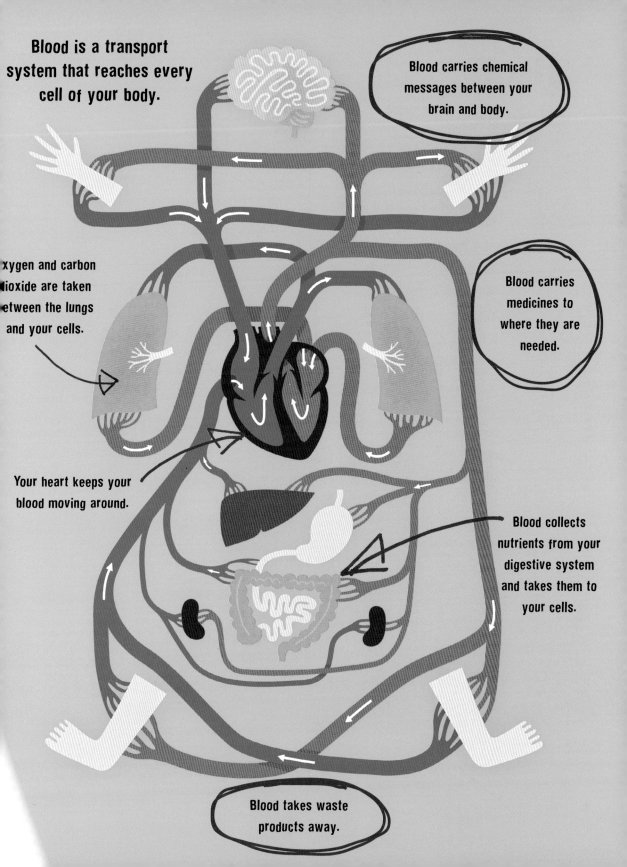

Heart

... in 30 seconds

The heart is one of the body's hardest-working parts. It's a muscly bag, about the size of your fist, which squeezes and relaxes to pump blood around the body.

Every minute, the heart squeezes or 'beats' about 70 times. That adds up to 4,200 times an hour, and around 100,000 times a day. It never stops, and never needs a rest.

Though the heart is very important, it's actually a simple organ. It has four spaces or chambers inside: two smaller ones called atriums, and two larger ones called ventricles. Large veins and arteries lead in and out of the heart to connect it to the body's network of blood vessels.

As the heart muscle relaxes, blood flows into the heart through the veins connected to it, and fills the chambers inside. The blood can only flow one way because the heart has valves that stop blood from flowing back the way it came. As the valves flap shut with each beat, they make a 'lub-dub' sound.

As the heart muscle squeezes, the blood is pushed out and into the arteries leading off to the rest of the body.

3-second sum-up

The heart beats 24 hours a day to pump blood around the body.

3-minute mission Take your pulse

1 Place three fingers on the inside of the wrist, just up from the thumb, where there is a large blood vessel. Can you feel a movement under your skin? That's called your pulse.

2 Use a watch or timer to count the number of beats in one minute. Your heart rate or pulse is how many times your heart beats in a minute.

The heart relaxes and opens up to fill with blood, then squeezes to pump the blood round your body as fast as you need it.

The heart muscle relaxes.

The heart fills with blood from the veins.

The heart muscle squeezes.

The heart pushes blood out into the arteries.

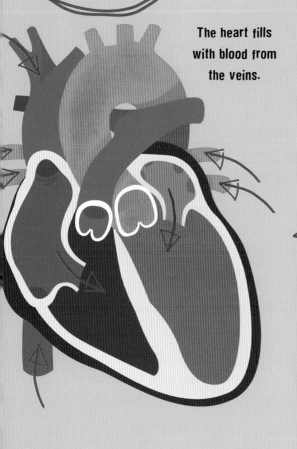

Your pulse speeds up to give you more energy when you need it.

Sprinting pulse – about 180 beats

Jogging pulse – about 140 beats

Walking pulse – about 95 beats

Resting pulse – about 70 beats

Immune system

... in 30 seconds

There's a constant battle going on in your body to keep germs and diseases OUT! The body system that fights this battle is called the immune system. It works in lots of ways.

Skin acts as a barrier against germs, and has an acidic coating that kills bacteria and mould. There are gaps in your skin for your eyes, nostrils, ears and mouth. But tears, mucus, earwax and saliva all contain germ-killing chemicals. If germs get into a cut, the immune system sends extra blood to the area. Special white blood cells attack and fight the germs.

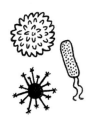

You often swallow germs, but saliva and strong stomach acid kill them. Some types, though, can get through and give you food poisoning. The immune system responds by causing vomiting and diarrhoea, to throw the germs out.

Cold and flu germs spread through the air. The immune system includes mucus in your nose, throat and lungs to trap the germs. If germs that cause disease invade the body, white blood cells often learn to destroy them by making chemicals called antibodies. That's why most people only get an illness such as chicken pox once.

3-second sum-up

The immune system works to fight germs and keep you healthy.

Feel your lymph nodes

Lymph nodes are small, bean-shaped parts of the immune system. Along with an organ called the spleen, they filter body fluid and catch germs. This is why if you're ill, your lymph nodes can swell up and feel sore because they have to catch lots of extra germs. You can sometimes feel the lymph nodes in your neck or armpits.

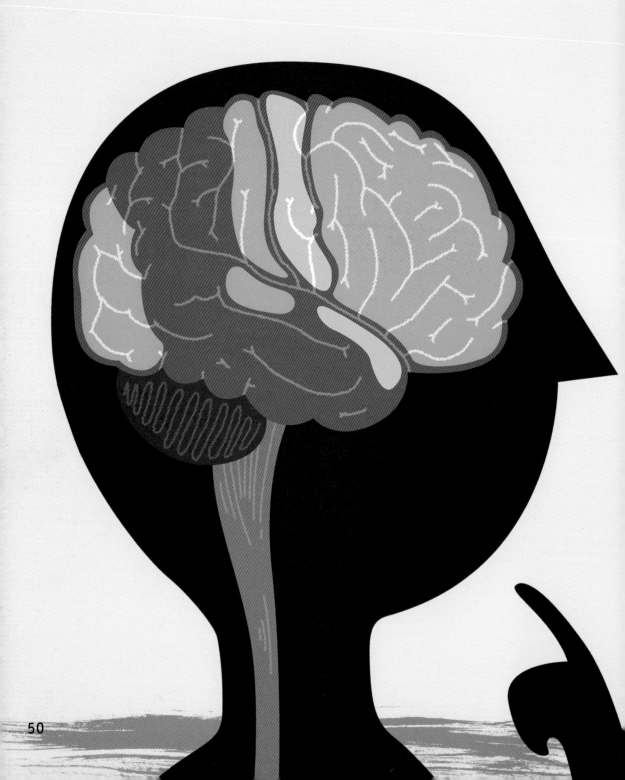

Brain and nervous system

How do you know what the words on this page mean? How can you make sense of things, think about the world and decide what to do? It's all thanks to your brilliant brain. Besides thinking, learning and remembering, it's in charge of running your body systems, processing sense signals and managing your muscles. Along with the nervous system, which links it to the rest of the body, your brain is in constant control.

Brain and nervous system
Glossary

brain stem The lower part of the brain that connects to the spinal cord. Many automatic functions are controlled here, such as keeping the heart beating, breathing and digesting food.

cerebellum The area of your brain that helps you to keep your balance and organize your body's movements. It means 'little brain'.

cerebrum The largest part of the brain, which is responsible for thoughts, feelings and senses such as touch, taste, smell and vision. It is what we use to think with.

cortex The outer layer of the **cerebrum**, which plays an important role in thinking.

hypothalamus A small brain part that does several jobs, including helping to control body temperature, hunger, thirst and sleep.

muscle A body part that contracts (gets shorter) to produce movement.

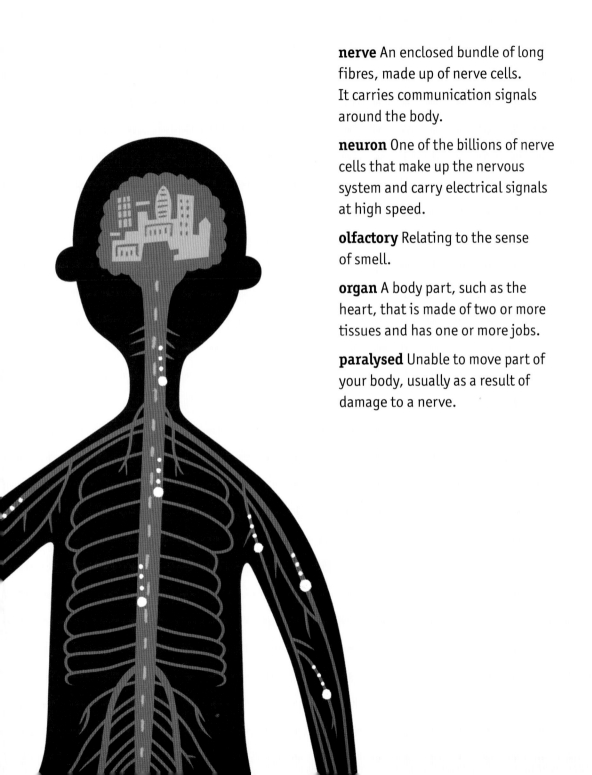

nerve An enclosed bundle of long fibres, made up of nerve cells. It carries communication signals around the body.

neuron One of the billions of nerve cells that make up the nervous system and carry electrical signals at high speed.

olfactory Relating to the sense of smell.

organ A body part, such as the heart, that is made of two or more tissues and has one or more jobs.

paralysed Unable to move part of your body, usually as a result of damage to a nerve.

Brain

... in 30 seconds

The brain is the most important organ of all. It's a living computer that controls your body. It collects signals from your senses to work out what's happening around you and it controls all your movements. It keeps track of what your organs are doing. It learns, thinks, remembers and makes decisions. Your brain is also where your mind is – your personality, ideas and feelings.

The human brain looks like a big, soft, wet, wrinkly, pinkish-grey walnut. The outside of the brain is made up of the cortex, where thinking and understanding happen. If you spread the cortex out flat, it would be as big as a pillowcase. But it's gathered up into lots of folds and creases so it can fit inside your head.

The brain is split into two halves. They are mostly separate from each other, but have a bundle of nerves called the corpus callosum linking them together. At the back of the brain is the cerebellum, a separate mini-brain that controls your movement and balance.

In the middle of the brain is the limbic system, a group of brain parts that deal with memory, fear, excitement and sleep.

3-second sum-up

The brain is a complex organ that controls the rest of the body.

3-minute mission Test your dominant side

Most people have a dominant side of the brain, which affects which side of the body they like to use. Try these activities – which side do you automatically use? Now try the other side!

- Hold a pair of scissors
- Throw or catch a ball
- Touch your nose
- Balance on one leg
- Kick a ball

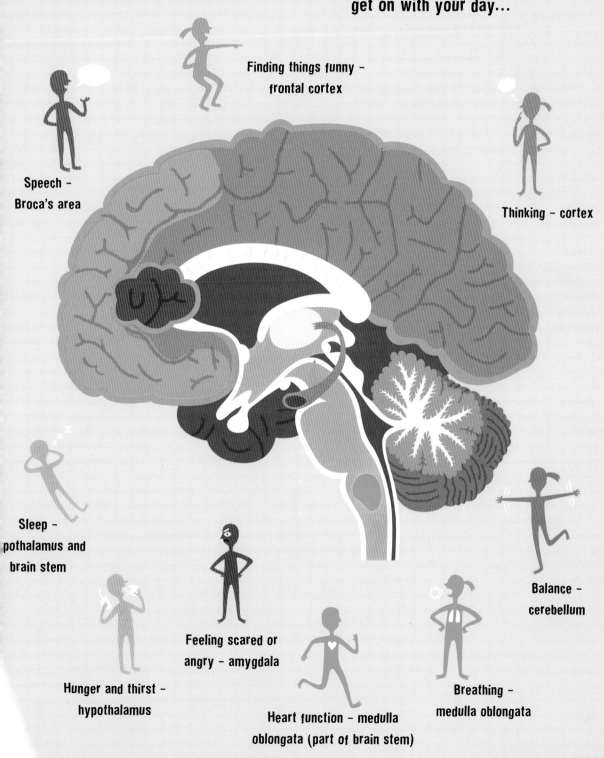

Thinking
... in 30 seconds

If you think about it, thinking is an amazing ability. You can imagine an elephant riding a bicycle while eating a birthday cake, even though you've never seen it! You can think about your earliest memories, the layout of your room, or your holiday plans. You can solve a maths problem, make up a story, or remember a dream you had. How does all this stuff 'happen' inside your brain?

The main thinking part of the brain, the cortex, is made up of billions of neurons, or nerve cells. Each neuron is like a tree with lots of tiny branches. The branches reach out and connect with other neurons. Wherever they connect, they almost touch, leaving a tiny gap.

Neurons pass signals to each other by sending chemicals across these gaps at lightning speed. All the time, signals are firing to and fro through your brain, along pathways made up of connected neurons. Different thoughts, ideas and decisions take different pathways through different parts of the cortex. As you learn and remember new stuff, you grow more branches and more connections.

3-second sum-up

Thinking happens when signals zoom along pathways in your brain.

3-minute mission Memory test

You need: • 10 small objects • A cloth • Tray or small table

Place the objects on a tray or table then ask a friend to look at them for 30 seconds. Then cover them with the cloth, and ask your friend to write down all the objects they can remember. Try the test on friends and family of different ages and see who does best!

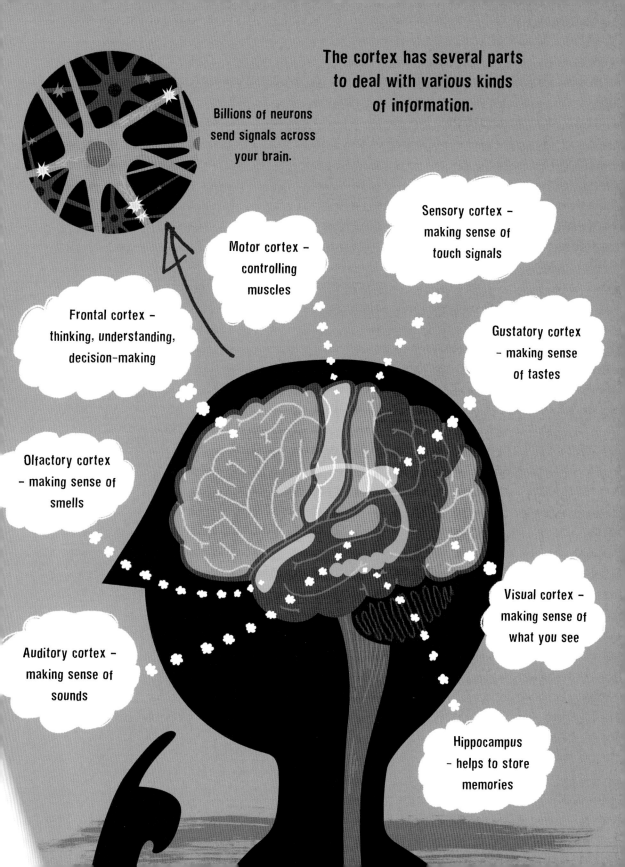

Nerves

... in 30 seconds

To do its job, the brain must be linked to every body part. The system that does this job is called the nervous system. It includes the brain and a huge network of nerves, made up of bundles of neurons, that lead all over the body.

The lowest part of the brain, the brain stem, is connected to the spinal cord, a major nerve highway leading down your back. It lies inside the vertebrae bones in the spine, protecting it from damage.

Nerves branch off from the spinal cord and lead down your arms and legs and into your fingers and toes. More nerves reach into organs, skin, bones and muscles all over the body. Some nerves collect sense signals and take them to the brain. Others carry signals from the brain to the muscles and body parts to make them work.

Neurons reaching to faraway body parts are the longest cells in the body. In a tall person, a neuron stretching between the spinal cord and the big toe could be over 1 m (3.3 ft) long! However, it's so thin that it is almost invisible.

3-second sum-up

A network of nerves links the brain to the rest of the body.

Spinal cord damage

If the spinal cord is damaged – for example, if you break your back or neck – it can stop signals getting through. This is why, after an accident, it's possible to be paralysed below the broken part of the spinal cord – from the waist down, for example. However, scientists are developing ways to reconnect damaged nerves in the spinal cord.

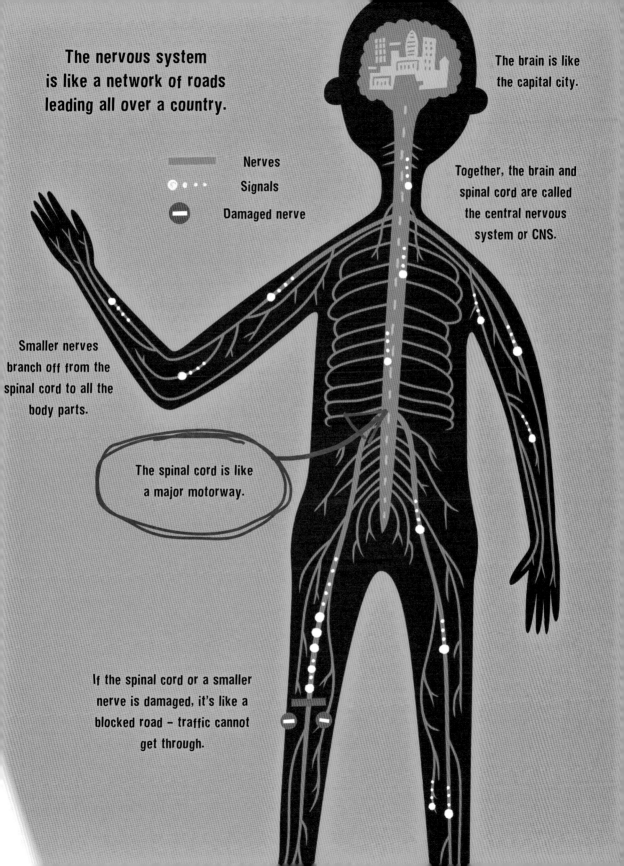

Sending signals

... in 30 seconds

Your nervous system is constantly dealing with thousands of signals. Nerves collect messages from all the senses at once and send a constant stream of signals to the brain. The brain processes them, working out what each signal means, and deciding what action to take. At the same time, it is sending out lots of signals to control all your body parts.

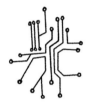

The brain is so big and complicated that it can handle all these different jobs at the same time. In fact, experts think a typical human brain can handle up to 100 trillion calculations every single second!

The messages and calculations happen so fast, we don't think about it. Even when you are just standing still, your body is constantly sending signals to your brain about its position and anything that affects it, such as the wind or holding something heavy. In response, the brain makes constant slight adjustments to your muscles so you stay upright.

3-second sum-up

Billions of signals are constantly zooming around your body and brain.

Synaesthesia

Synaesthesia (say sin-uhs-THEE-zhee-uh), meaning 'together sensing', is a strange brain condition that affects around 2 per cent of people. If you have it, your senses get mixed up. For example, sounds seem to have colours, or tastes seem to have shapes. For some synaesthetic people, numbers, letters and days of the week can have colours, or even personalities. Synaesthesia may be caused by signals between parts of the nervous system that aren't normally connected.

Your brain works like a computer circuit board by processing information and sending signals.

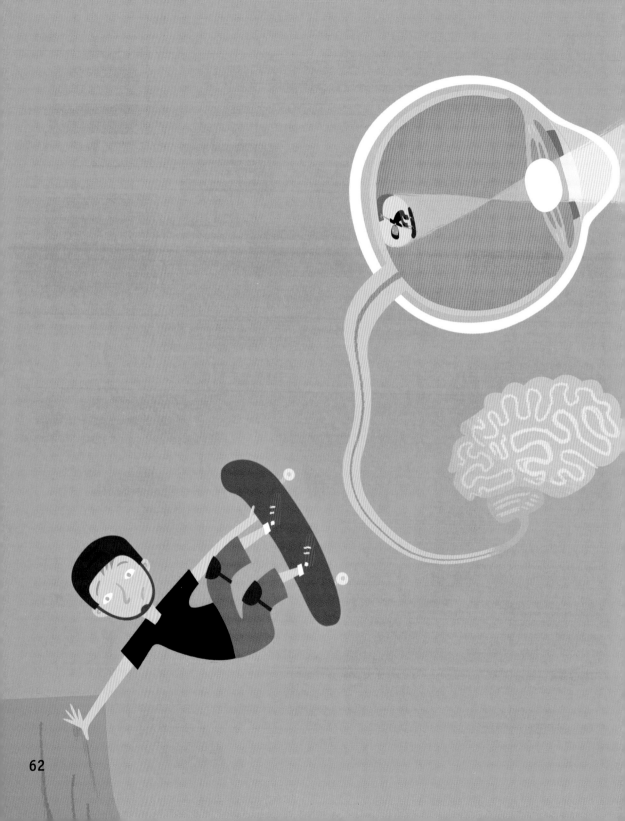

Senses

Imagine life without your five senses – sight, hearing, taste, smell and touch. It's impossible! Your senses tell you what's happening and send information to your brain. They keep you in contact with the world so you can learn and experience things and store away memories to refer to later. And, every day, you use them to help you find your way around, detect danger, and deal with other people, objects and tasks.

Senses
Glossary

cochlea A small, curled tube in the inner ear. The cochlea is filled with liquid, which is set into motion, like a wave, when other parts of the ear vibrate.

lens A clear and colourless jelly-like structure that focuses light rays on the back of the eyeball.

molecule Two or more atoms (tiny particles) joined together.

olfactory Relating to the sense of smell.

ossicle One of the three tiniest, most delicate bones in your body, which help sound move along on its journey into the inner ear.

papilla (plural: papillae) A name for a small bump or sticking-out body part. The papillae on the tongue contain taste buds.

proprioception The ability to sense the position, location and movement of the body and its parts.

retina Part at the back of the eye that turns light rays into signals that our brain can understand. The retina uses light-sensitive cells called rods and cones to see.

semicircular canal One of three small loops above the **cochlea**. They are filled with liquid and have thousands of tiny hairs that sense movement, helping you to balance.

sensor A cell that detects things you touch and then sends information to the brain.

vibration A slight shaking movement that makes something tremble or wobble.

Seeing

... in 30 seconds

Seeing is one of our most useful senses. It lets us detect everything around us in a split second, by sensing the light that comes from objects.

Each eyeball collects rays of light coming from objects. The rays pass through the cornea, a clear window at the front, and enter the pupil, the little black hole in the middle. Then they pass through a clear, jelly-like lens. The lens helps to bend and focus the rays so that they form a clear image on the retina, an area of light-sensing cells at the back of the eyeball.

Because light travels in straight lines, the light rays cross over each other as they enter the eye, ending up in the opposite position. So the image that hits the retina is upside down and back to front.

Millions of cells in the retina detect the patterns of light that fall on them, sending signals along the optic nerve to the brain. The brain turns the image the right way up and makes sense of what it can see.

3-second sum-up

Eyes collect light, sense the patterns it makes and send signals to the brain.

3-minute mission Trick your brain!

The brain sometimes gets things wrong. Test yourself with this amazing illusion:

Are these two tabletops a different size and shape, or the same?

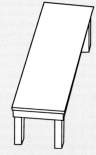

Answer on page 96

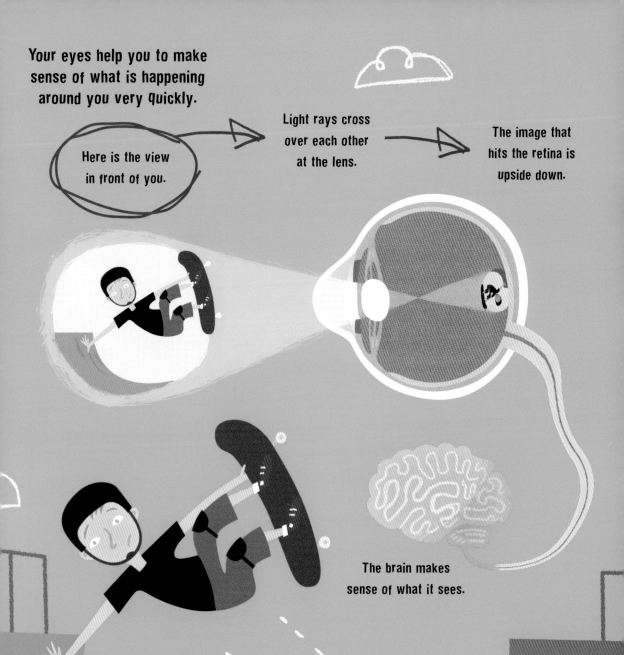

Your eyes help you to make sense of what is happening around you very Quickly.

Here is the view in front of you.

Light rays cross over each other at the lens.

The image that hits the retina is upside down.

The brain makes sense of what it sees.

The upside-down image is turned the right way up by the brain.

Hearing
... in 30 seconds

On the sides of your head there are two curly flaps sticking out, which you probably call your ears. But there's much more to ears than this! They actually reach deep inside your head.

The ears' job is to collect sounds from the air. We are surrounded by sounds. Objects moving and scraping, music playing and people talking all make the molecules in the air vibrate. These vibrations spread out through the air. If they reach your ears, they set off a chain reaction.

First, your outer ear (the flappy bit) collects the vibrations and directs them into the ear canal, or earhole. When they hit the tightly stretched eardrum, it vibrates. The vibrations are passed on through three tiny bones inside the ear, and into a snail-shaped, fluid-filled chamber called the cochlea. It contains tiny hairs that pick up the vibrations and send signals to the brain.

The brain receives a pattern of varying signals that represent the varying speed and strength of the sound vibrations. By comparing them to its memories, it works out what you can hear – the sound of a car horn, your favourite song or a friend yelling your name.

3-second sum-up

Ears collect sounds from the air and send signals to your brain.

3-minute mission Make an eardrum

You need: • Clingfilm • Bowl • Uncooked rice or sugar • Pan lid • Wooden spoon

1 Stretch the clingfilm tightly over the bowl. Put a few grains of rice or sugar on the clingfilm.

2 Make a loud noise close to the clingfilm (but not touching it), by banging the pan lid with the spoon. The sound should make the clingfilm 'eardrum' vibrate, and you will see the rice or sugar jump. This is how eardrums vibrate when sound hits them.

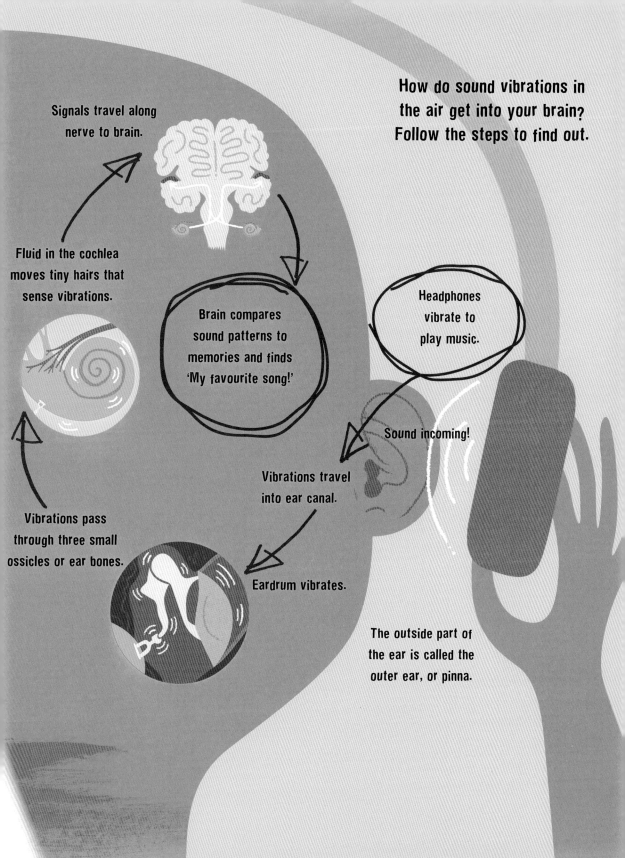

Smelling

... in 30 seconds

If your nose is working well, you can detect up to a trillion different smells! But your nose is quite small, and so is the smell-detecting part of the brain. So how do you do it?

Smells form because tiny molecules break free from most substances, and float off into the air. Whether it's freshly baked bread, hot coffee, clean washing or a stinky overflowing bin, you can smell it because tiny bits of the smelly stuff actually float up your nose!

High up inside your nose are special smell-detecting cells. Different types of these cells can detect different types of molecules. Often, a smell contains a mixture of substances, and this triggers several different smell detectors. The detectors send signals into the brain, and the brain works out what the smell is, by comparing the signal to its bank of smell records.

Some things, such as a gold coin, don't smell of anything at all. Why? Because some substances, such as gold, are very stable. This means molecules don't easily break off from them, so there's nothing to get up your nose.

3-second sum-up

Smell detectors inside your nose detect tiny bits of substances around you.

Smells and feelings

Answer these questions:

• Which smell reminds you of being tiny?

• Which smell reminds you of a great holiday?

• How does a really bad smell make you feel?

Your sense of smell is closely linked to brain parts that deal with emotions and memories. This may be why smells can bring back memories from long ago or create strong feelings.

Your sense of smell is triggered
when molecules float into the air
and are sniffed up your nose.

It is linked to part of the brain
called the olfactory bulb.

From here, signals travel to
other parts of the brain.

The olfactory epithelium
contains the smell-
detecting nerve endings.

The brain decodes the signals.
'Mmmm! Fresh coffee!'
'Urggh! Stinky bin!'

Tasting
... in 30 seconds

One of the things that makes food so enjoyable is your sense of taste. Your tongue tastes things using sense organs called taste buds.

Stick your tongue out and look at it in a mirror, and you'll see that it has tiny bumps all over it. However, these bumps are not taste buds. They are called papillae. The taste buds themselves are much smaller, and are found inside little gaps surrounding the papillae.

When you chew food, your mouth releases saliva, or spit. This helps tiny amounts of the food to wash down into the gaps around the papillae, and touch the taste buds. Each taste bud contains about 50 taste-detecting cells that can sense several different basic tastes: salty, sweet, sour, bitter and umami, or savoury. They send signals to the brain, which works out what the combination of signals means, and what the taste is.

Your sense of smell is also very important for tasting food. The smell of the food wafts up your nose and gives you a lot of information about it. That's why having a bad cold and a blocked nose makes it harder to taste things properly.

3-second sum-up

You taste using your tongue – and your nose as well!

3-minute mission Taste test

You need: • Small piece of apple • Small piece of cabbage • Small piece of carrot • Blindfold

How well can you taste without your nose? Blindfold some friends or family members and ask them to hold their noses. Then let them taste the three pieces of food. Can they tell which is which? Let them try again without holding their noses.

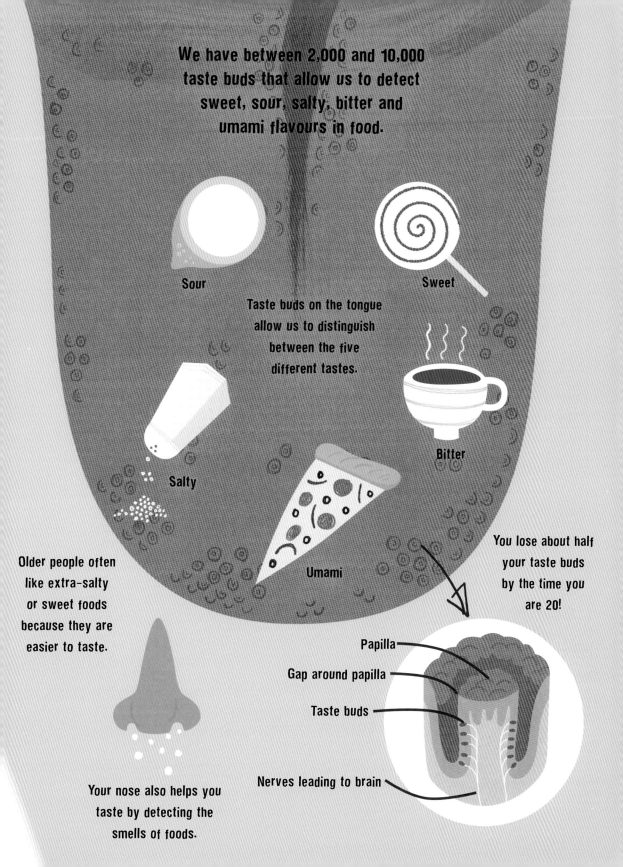

We have between 2,000 and 10,000 taste buds that allow us to detect sweet, sour, salty, bitter and umami flavours in food.

Sour

Sweet

Taste buds on the tongue allow us to distinguish between the five different tastes.

Salty

Bitter

Umami

Older people often like extra-salty or sweet foods because they are easier to taste.

You lose about half your taste buds by the time you are 20!

Papilla

Gap around papilla

Taste buds

Nerves leading to brain

Your nose also helps you taste by detecting the smells of foods.

Touch

... in 30 seconds

While seeing, hearing, tasting and smelling all happen in your head, your sense of touch is all over your body.

Under your skin's surface, and inside many of your body parts and organs, are millions of touch sensors, linked to nerves that lead to your brain. When something triggers a touch sensor, it sends a signal to your brain about what you can feel.

You might not think of touch as a very important sense, but in fact it's vital. It helps us move around, hold objects, type on a keyboard and get dressed. Imagine not being able to feel your feet on the floor, a shower or a hug! But most important of all, touch warns us of danger. Pain isn't nice, but it's very useful – it lets you know you have a cut, or a twisted ankle or that something is burning you, so that you can take action.

There are several different types of touch sensor:

• Pressure – detects pressure, vibrations and textures.

• Pain – tells your brain when something harms your skin.

• Temperature – detects heat, cold and temperature changes.

3-second sum-up

Touch sensors in your body detect pressure, pain, heat and cold.

3-minute mission Tongue trick!

Hold up a fork vertically and press the tip of your tongue against the prongs. Most people find the fork feels bent, even though it's not. As with other senses, your brain makes assumptions about what you can feel. It knows your tongue has a rounded shape at the tip. If your tongue can feel four objects, the brain decides they must be in a curved pattern.

Where am I?

... in 30 seconds

You probably don't think about it, but at any moment, your brain knows your body's position in space. This is thanks to a special type of touch sense, called proprioception (say pro-pree-o-sep-shun).

Proprioception helps your brain control your movements. You need it for all your everyday activities, such as walking and running, catching a ball and turning over in bed. Your brain can only send your body instructions about what to do next because it knows where all your body parts are.

Proprioception works using sensors in your muscles and joints. They constantly send signals to your brain about where all your body parts are, the positions they are in and how fast they are moving.

At the same time, ear parts called semicircular canals, close to the cochlea, help you stay balanced. The canals are filled with thick liquid that swirls and sloshes around when you turn around, lean over or turn upside down.

3-second sum-up

Proprioception and balance help your brain control your body's movements.

3-minute mission Test your body

Try these balance and proprioception tests.

• Close your eyes and stretch your arms out to your sides. Then try to place both index fingers right on the end of your nose.

• Find a line along the floor, such as a gap between floorboards. Walk along it, putting one foot right in front of the other. How fast can you go without falling off the line?

• Lift one foot off the ground, and close your eyes. How long can you balance like that?

Your amazing body

Your body doesn't just keep itself going – it also changes. It gets bigger and bigger as you grow from a baby into an adult. Then, it's ready to do something even more amazing: reproduce and make copies of itself, or in other words, have babies. The way the human body grows and changes, and can pass on its qualities to new human beings, is decided by the DNA found deep inside our body cells.

Glossary

base One of the four main chemicals that make up **DNA**.

chromosome A long, coiled-up strand of **DNA** found inside the **nucleus** of a **cell**. Chromosomes carry the **genes**.

cell One of the tiny units that living things are made of. Some organisms, such as bacteria, are made up of a single cell, while others are made up of trillions of cells.

DNA Short for deoxyribonucleic acid. DNA is the material that **genes** are made from. It forms long, thin strands in a shape similar to a spiral ladder.

egg The female reproductive **cell**, or gamete.

fertilization The joining of a male gamete (**sperm**) and female gamete (**egg**) to make a new cell that can grow into a baby.

gene A section of a **DNA** strand inside a **cell nucleus**, which contains instructions for cells to follow.

growth plate The region in a long bone where it grows longer.

hair follicle A small, cup-shaped part in the skin's surface from which a hair grows.

muscle A body part that contracts (gets shorter) to produce movement.

neuron One of the billions of nerve cells that make up the nervous system and carry electrical signals at high speed.

nucleus The core at the centre of a **cell**. It acts like the brain of the cell and controls the way the cell works.

ovary One of two female reproductive organs that make and store **egg cells**.

saliva A liquid that is released from glands in the mouth to help you taste and dissolve food.

sperm The male reproductive **cell**, or gamete.

testicle One of two egg-shaped glands in the scrotum (the sac that hangs under the penis) that make **sperm**.

Reproduction

... in 30 seconds

Reproduction means making copies, and all types of living things can make copies of themselves. For animals, including humans, that means having babies.

It's amazing to think that our bodies can actually make whole, new, complicated human beings. Every single one of us started out as one cell from our mother's body and one cell from our father's. These combined to make a new cell that grew into a human being.

The special cells that make babies are called reproductive cells, and they are made in the reproductive system. Men and women have different reproductive systems.

Men make sperm in their testicles and women have ovaries that release female reproductive cells, or eggs. When an egg joins with a sperm, the new cell moves to the womb, where it can grow into a baby. It takes nine months for a baby to grow inside a pregnant woman's womb, before being born.

3-second sum-up

To make a baby, male and female reproductive cells need to join together.

In the lab

Reproductive cells don't have to meet inside a woman's body – scientists have found that they can collect egg and sperm cells and join them together in a container. This is known as In-Vitro Fertilization, or IVF. The new cell can then be placed in a woman's womb to grow. Doctors sometimes use this method to help people have babies.

Everyone who has ever lived was made by combining a cell from a woman with a cell from a man.

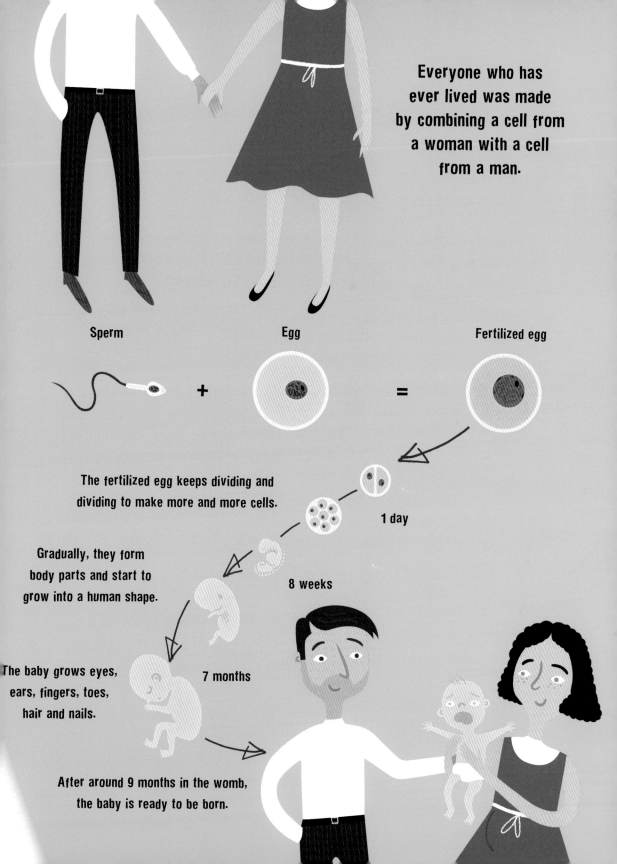

Sperm

+

Egg

=

Fertilized egg

The fertilized egg keeps dividing and dividing to make more and more cells.

1 day

Gradually, they form body parts and start to grow into a human shape.

8 weeks

The baby grows eyes, ears, fingers, toes, hair and nails.

7 months

After around 9 months in the womb, the baby is ready to be born.

Growing

... in 30 seconds

Of course, the growing doesn't stop once a baby is born – that's just the beginning!

Out of all animals, humans are among the slowest to become adults. Humans are intelligent, and a lot of what we do is based on learning. It takes a long time to learn all the things we need to know.

In the first year, a baby learns how to deal with all the different information from its senses, and how to control its body. By about 12 months, babies start learning to walk and talk.

Children get taller as their bones grow. Arm and leg bones have special growth plates where new bone is formed. Other bones, such as the skull, grow by breaking down old bone and building new bone. At the age of about five, milk teeth begin to fall out, to be replaced by full-sized adult teeth.

From about 11 to 18, humans go through adolescence. They begin to grow an adult body. When you're a teenager, your brain also changes a lot – its neuron pathways become more fixed into adult patterns.

3-second sum-up

It takes at least 20 years for a human to grow into an adult.

3-minute mission Growing time

It takes a human about 20 years to reach full adult size. Match the animal to the time it takes to become an adult.

Honeybee	3 years
Bottlenose dolphin	5 years
Giant tortoise	14 years
Golden eagle	25 years
Dragonfly	21 days

Answer on page 96

Your body changes a lot as you grow up, and you get MUCH taller as your bones get longer.

In long bones, such as the ones in your legs, new growth forms in the growth plates and pushes away from them, making the bone get longer and longer.

Bone growth plate

180

160

140

120

100

Age: 15
Height: 170 cm
(5 ft 7 inches)
You'll be nearing your full adult height. Your body gets stronger as well as taller.

Age 7
Height: 130 cm
(4 ft 3 inches)
You have much longer limbs and your head takes up less of your height.

Age: 3
Height: 104 cm (3 ft 5 inches)
You're about 60% of your adult height.

Ageing

... in 30 seconds

You can often make a rough guess about how old someone is. That's because as we get older, our bodies change.

This happens because our cells cannot keep living and replacing themselves for ever. Slowly, some cells start to die off or stop working. For example, hair goes grey as we lose the hair root cells that make hair colour. Sometimes, hair follicles stop working too, making people go bald. Joints wear down and work less well, and bones and muscles get thinner.

Wrinkles happen because as people get older, skin cells grow less quickly. This means the skin gets thinner and can't repair damage very well. In places where your skin moves a lot – especially the face, which we use for talking, eating and expressing feelings – the skin starts to form permanent folds.

Luckily, technology means that we can fix a lot of the problems of ageing. Glasses, hearing aids and even surgery to improve eye lenses or replace a hip joint, mean many people can keep being active, healthy and happy in old age.

3-second sum-up

As humans get older, some cells die off, causing ageing.

Older and older!

You might not like the idea of getting old, but at least we are living longer than we used to. Worldwide, the average human lifespan has risen from less than 40 in 1900, to almost 70 today! This is mainly thanks to a better supply of healthy food, better medicines and warmer, safer homes.

Genes and DNA

... in 30 seconds

All living things have genes that control the way their cells work – and so control how they live and grow. But what are genes, and what is DNA?

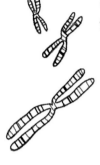

If you could look inside a typical human body cell, you would find a nucleus, the cell's control centre. Inside the nucleus are 46 coiled-up strands, called chromosomes. The chromosomes are made of a chemical called DNA, which forms a long, stringy shape similar to a thin, twisted ladder. DNA is made up of four chemicals called bases.

A gene is a section of DNA, containing a particular sequence of bases. The bases act as a kind of code that the cell can understand and follow, like a set of instructions. Each gene tells the cell how to make something the body needs – including new cells and body parts, and body substances such as hair or saliva.

Most cells have a complete set of chromosomes and genes, but they only use the genes they need for their own particular jobs. So, as hair follicle cells need to make hair, they follow the genes that contain hair-making instructions.

3-second sum-up

Genes are made of DNA, and contain instructions for cells to follow.

How long are your chromosomes?

• If the chromosomes in one cell were uncoiled and stretched out, they would total around 2 m (6 ft) long.

• Your body contains around 100 trillion cells, and most of them contain a full set of chromosomes.

• If all the chromosomes in your body were stretched out, they would reach 200 BILLION km (124 billion miles). That's the distance to the Sun and back, 70 times!

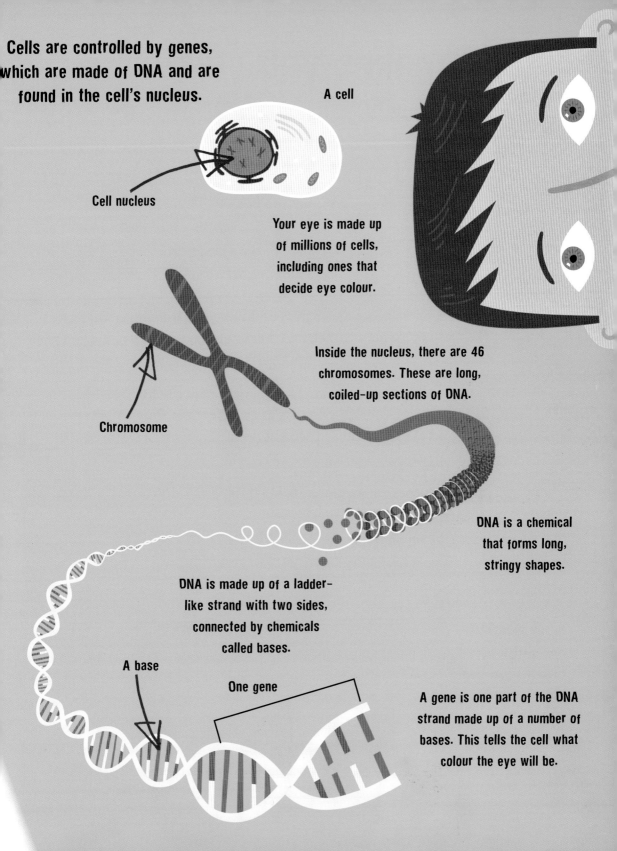

Cells are controlled by genes, which are made of DNA and are found in the cell's nucleus.

A cell

Cell nucleus

Your eye is made up of millions of cells, including ones that decide eye colour.

Chromosome

Inside the nucleus, there are 46 chromosomes. These are long, coiled-up sections of DNA.

DNA is a chemical that forms long, stringy shapes.

DNA is made up of a ladder-like strand with two sides, connected by chemicals called bases.

A base

One gene

A gene is one part of the DNA strand made up of a number of bases. This tells the cell what colour the eye will be.

What makes you you?

... in 30 seconds

Though there are around 7 billion other humans on the planet, no one is quite like you. You have your own appearance, way of walking, likes and dislikes. What makes you who you are? Well, partly it's your genes.

Each species of living thing has its own genome, or set of genes. As you're human, you have a human genome. It makes you grow into a human shape, with human features and human abilities such as walking and talking.

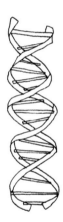

But everyone's genes are slightly different. This is because whenever a living thing makes a new cell, that cell gets its own copy of the genome. The copying doesn't always work perfectly, so mistakes can creep in.

This is why people have different hair, eye and skin colours, heights and facial features – qualities known as genetic traits. Parents pass on combinations of their traits to their children. That's why a feature such as ginger hair can run in families.

However, it's not just your genes that make you you. Things you experience and learn are also important – such as how much food and sunlight you get, and experiences such as playing an instrument.

3-second sum-up

You are a unique mixture of your genes ('nature') and experiences ('nurture').

Identical twins

Identical twins start off as one cell which then splits into two. This means they have the exact same DNA to start with, and are as alike as two people can be. However, they have their own personalities, and the DNA in their cells gradually changes over time. Also, they have different fingerprints because their patterns are shaped when their fingers touch things in the womb. So even if you're an identical twin, you're still one of a kind.

our unique set of genes
makes you different from
everyone else.

Your natural hair colour
and curliness are decided
by DNA.

Identical twins have the
same DNA but they have
their own personalities.

Having ginger hair is
a genetic trait.

The way you are brought
up also affects the person
you become.

Genes are made of DNA, which is
a double helix shape - a bit like a
spiral-shaped rollercoaster.

Discover more

BOOKS

Blood, Bones and Body Bits (Horrible Science) by Nick Arnold **(Scholastic, 2008)**

Body: An Amazing Tour of Human Anatomy by Robert Winston **(Dorling Kindersley, 2005)**

Can You Lick Your Own Elbow? And Other Questions About the Human Body by Paul Mason **(Raintree, 2014)**

A Day Trip Inside the Human Body by Claire Throp **(Raintree, 2015)**

The Everything® KIDS' Human Body Book: All You Need to Know About Your Body Systems – From Head to Toe! by Sheri Amsel **(Adams Media Corporation, 2012)**

First Encyclopedia of the Human Body (Usborne First Encyclopedias) by Fiona Chandler and David Hancock **(Usborne Publishing Ltd, 2011)**

Human Body A Children's Encyclopedia (DK Reference) **(Dorling Kindersley, 2012)**

Let's Talk About Sex by Robie Harris **(Walker Books Ltd, 2010)**

Look Inside: Your Body (Usborne Look Inside) by Louie Stowell **(Usborne Publishing Ltd, 2012)**

Slide and Discover: Human Body by Barbara Taylor **(Silver Dolphin, 2014)**

Ultimate Bodypedia: An Amazing Inside-Out Tour of the Human Body by Patricia Daniels, Christina Wilson and Anne Schreiber **(National Geographic Society, 2014)**

The Way We Work **by David Macaulay (Walker, 2009)**

Your Body: Inside and Out: Bones and Muscles by Angela Royston **(Franklin Watts, 2015)**

DVDS

Rock n Learn Human Body
(Quantum Leap Group, 2012) Suitable for all ages.

Inside the Human Body **(BBC, 2011)** PG.

Incredible Human Machine **(National Geographic, 2010)**
Suitable for all ages.

The Human Body **(BBC, 2012)** PG.

WEBSITES

Easy Science for Kids: Human Body
http://easyscienceforkids.com/human-body/
Simple information about your senses, body systems, brain, growing
up and healthy food

How the Body Works
http://kidshealth.org/kid/htbw/#cat20183
Articles on the human body as well as quizzes, activities and
word searches

Rader's Biology4Kids!
http://www.biology4kids.com/
Information on cells and microorganisms, as well as how body
systems work

The Human Body
*http://www.kidskonnect.com/subjectindex/31-educational/
health/337-human-body.html*
Fascinating facts on the human body and short movies to watch

The Body and Medicines
*http://www.childrensuniversity.manchester.ac.uk/interactives/
science/bodyandmedicine/*
Interactive website on the human body

Human Body
*http://science.nationalgeographic.com/science/health-and-human-
body/human-body/*
An interactive website looking at the brain, heart, lungs, skin and
digestive system

Index

Quiz answers

page 16: organ quiz

Kidney – Filters waste out of blood
Heart – Pumps blood
Oesophagus – Carries food from throat
    to stomach
Lung – Extracts oxygen from air
Lymph node – Traps germs
Larynx – Makes voice sounds

page 66: table trick

They are the same! Try measuring them
with a ruler so you can see!

page 84: how much growing

Honeybee – 21 days
Bottlenose dolphin – 14 years
Giant tortoise – 25 years
Golden eagle – 5 years
Dragonfly – 3 years